God and the Egg

1+1+1=1

JANETTA MAXWELL

Trilogy Christian Publishers
A Wholly Owned Subsidiary of Trinity Broadcasting Network
2442 Michelle Drive
Tustin, CA 92780

Copyright © 2023 by Janetta Maxwell

All rights reserved, including the right to reproduce this book or portions thereof in any form whatsoever.

For information, address Trilogy Christian Publishing
Rights Department, 2442 Michelle Drive, Tustin, Ca 92780.
Trilogy Christian Publishing/ TBN and colophon are trademarks of Trinity Broadcasting Network.

For information about special discounts for bulk purchases, please contact Trilogy Christian Publishing.

Manufactured in the United States of America

Trilogy Disclaimer: The views and content expressed in this book are those of the author and may not necessarily reflect the views and doctrine of Trilogy Christian Publishing or the Trinity Broadcasting Network.

10 9 8 7 6 5 4 3 2 1

Library of Congress Cataloging-in-Publication Data is available.

ISBN 979-8-88738-272-2 (Print Book)
ISBN 979-8-88738-273-9 (ebook)

Dedication

To Maddek: thank you for being a faithful servant to the Lord. It brings so much joy to my heart to have you be my helper each week in Sunday school. Continue serving God, and He will direct your path.

It was a beautiful, warm, sunny summer afternoon. A young boy named Maddek was sitting at the kitchen table at his grandma's house, eating lunch.

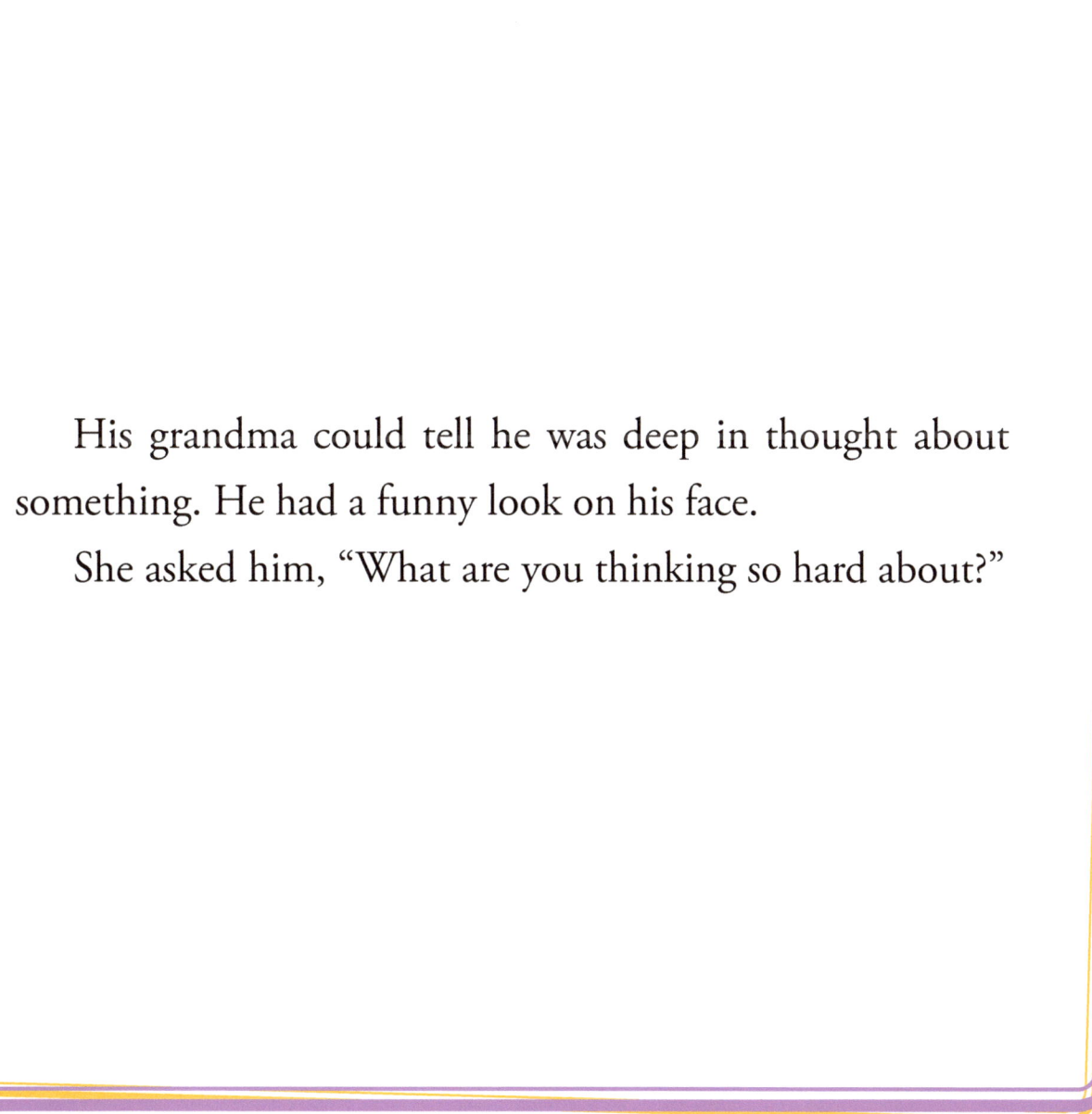

His grandma could tell he was deep in thought about something. He had a funny look on his face.

She asked him, "What are you thinking so hard about?"

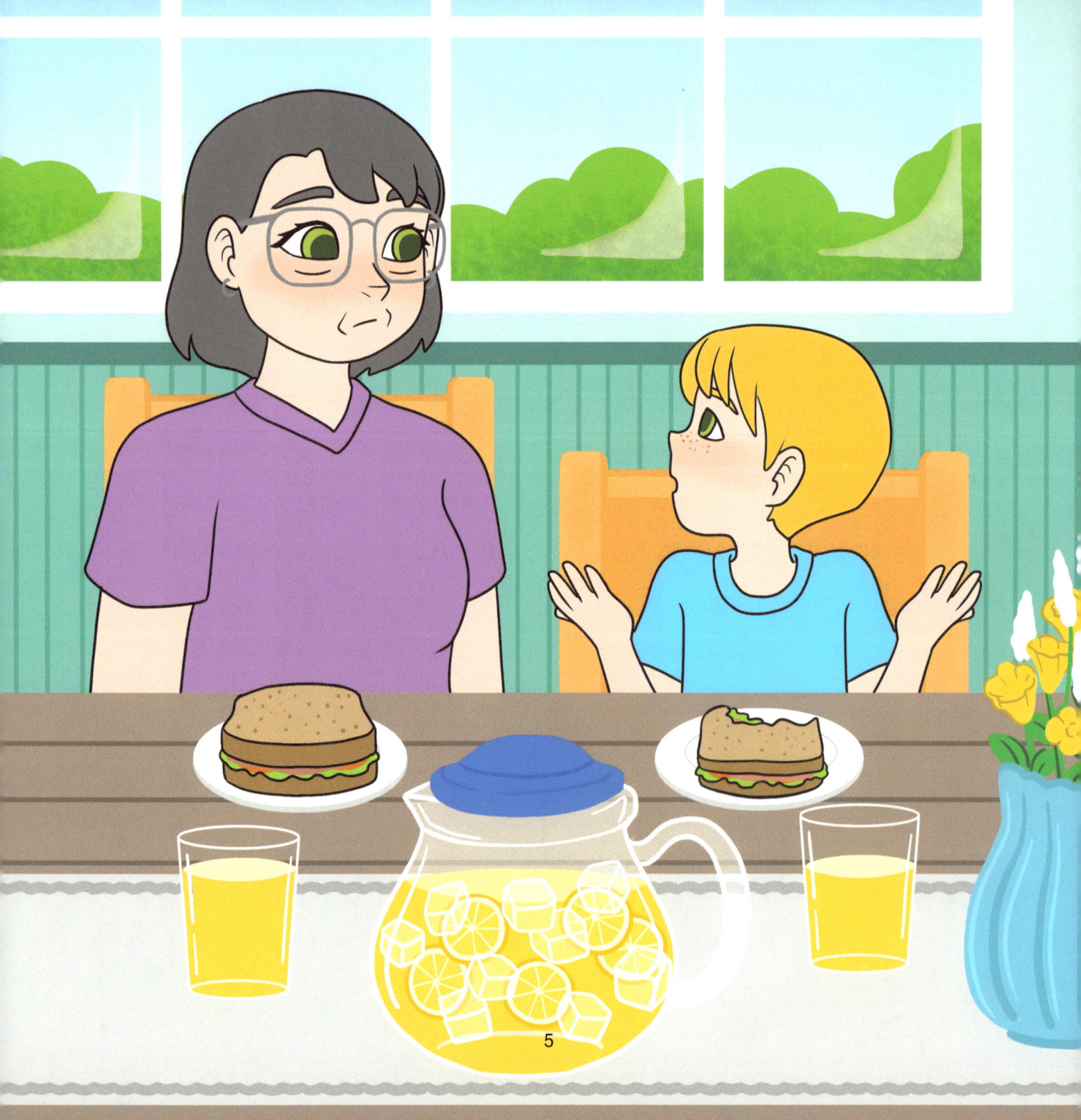

Maddek looked at his grandma and said, "My Sunday school teacher said that God the Father, Jesus, and the Holy Spirit are all three separate individuals, yet they are all one! She read 1 John 5:7 (KJV), 'For there are three that bear record in heaven, the Father, the Word, and the Holy Ghost: and these three are one.' She called it the 'Trinity'; I call it confusing!"

Maddek's grandma looked at him and gave him that special grandma smile and said, "Come outside and help me with my chores, and I will explain it to you."

Maddek looked at her and sighed, "I really don't think you're going to do any better than my Sunday school teacher! It's very confusing!"

"Maybe," grandma said, "but let me give it the ole grandma try?"

"Okay, fine," said Maddek, as he rolled his eyes and shook his head back and forth.

Now Maddek's grandma had a beautiful farm. She had so many different animals. There were cows, horses, ducks, and sheep. But his favorite were the baby chickens. They were so soft and fuzzy! He loved to pick them up and hold them in his hands and pet the tops of their heads. He loved all the animals, and helping to take care of them was always a lot of work, but so much fun.

As they walked into the barn where the chickens lived, grandma kneeled down and picked up an egg. She looked at Maddek and asked him, "What do you see?"

Maddek said, "An egg."

Grandma said, "Yes, but what else do you see when you look at an egg?"

Maddek said, "Breakfast."

Grandma giggled and smiled at him and said, "Do you know what I see? I see life, and all life begins as an egg, but I also see the Trinity."

Then grandma asked, "How many parts are there to an egg?"

Maddek answered, "There are three.

The hard outer shell, the white part (albumen) of the egg, and in the center is the yolk. The hard shell on the outside of the egg protects it, and the white part of the egg acts as a cushioning between the shell and the yolk. But the yolk is where all the protein and essential nutrients are located. All three parts make up the one egg! Just like the Trinity."

The Trinity is made up of three parts: God the Father, God the Son, and God the Holy Spirit. Think of the Holy Spirit as the outer shell, protecting you all day.

Then there is Jesus—He is the white part of the egg, acting as a cushion between God and the Holy Spirit.

Next is God; He is the yolk, the beginning of all life. You can't get to the yolk without going through the hard outer shell and the white part of the egg.

Just like you can't get to God the Father without going through the Holy Spirit and Jesus.

Just like all three parts of the egg make up one egg, all three parts of the Trinity make up one God.

About the Author

Janetta Maxwell and her husband blended their families together over twenty years ago. She is a mother of three boys and has eight grandchildren: five girls and three boys. Not only are they a blended family, but they are also a multi-racial family. She loves teaching all of them about Christ, bringing the Bible to life in ways that children can understand. When she was a child, she made a profession of faith, but it wasn't until she was a young adult that she accepted Christ as her Savior. She enjoys serving in her local church, teaching Sunday school. Recently, God called her to share her Bible stories with others.

Her church has a motto: "Love God, Love People." It is something she truly believes and tries to live by.

She prays this story will be a blessing to you and your family.

CPSIA information can be obtained
at www.ICGtesting.com
Printed in the USA
BVHW011747220223
659019BV00002B/4